Quick

Itty Bitties

Indulge in color with Bonbons®, the Lion Brand® Yarn Company collections of 8 miniature balls of yarn. Each collection includes 8 shades in an assortment of mercerized cotton, acrylic, or metallic. Available in an array of colors, Bonbons are perfect for any project requiring multiple colors, such as amigurumi, colorwork, embroidery, and embellishments. They're also great for friendship bracelets and kids' crafts, and make adorable gifts.

About Lion Brand® Yarn Company

Lion Brand® Yarn Company is a family-owned and operated business and a beloved American brand since 1878. Throughout its history, Lion Brand Yarn has been at the forefront of yarn trends while consistently providing its customers with the highest quality product at a value price. The company's mission is to provide ideas, inspiration and education to yarn crafters.

LEISURE ARTS, INC.
Maumelle, Arkansas

CHILD'S EARFLAP HAT

EASY

SIZE

Finished Circumference:

About 17" (43 cm), will stretch to fit a range of sizes.

Finished Height:

About 7" (18 cm), not including Earflaps

SHOPPING LIST

Yarn (Light Weight) LIGHT 3

LION BRAND® BONBONS® (Art. #601)

- ☐ #610 Brights - 1 pack **or** color of your choice

Crochet Hook

LION BRAND® crochet hook

- ☐ Size H-8 (5 mm)

  or size needed for gauge

Additional Supplies

- ☐ LION BRAND® stitch markers
- ☐ LION BRAND® Pom-Pom Maker
- ☐ LION BRAND® large-eyed blunt needle

GAUGE

16 sc + 20 rnds = 4" (10 cm).

BE SURE TO CHECK YOUR GAUGE.

STITCH GUIDE

SINGLE CROCHET 2 TOGETHER (abbreviated sc2tog)

(Insert hook in next st and draw up a loop) 2 times, yarn over and draw through all 3 loops on hook – 1 st decreased.

NOTES

1. Hat is worked in the round. Do not turn at the ends of rnds.
2. Earflaps are worked back and forth in rows across lower edge of Hat.
3. Color is changed every other rnd/row.

COLORS

Purple (A)	Orange (E)
Yellow (B)	Turquoise (F)
Orange-Red (C)	Pink (G)
Lime (D)	Magenta (H)

HAT

With A, ch 70; taking care not to twist ch, join with sl st in first ch to form a ring.

Rnd 1 (RS): Ch 1, sc in same ch as joining and in each ch around; join with sl st in first sc – 70 sc. Fasten off.

Note: Work designated sts through back loop and other sts through both loops.

Rnd 2: From RS, join B with sc in back loop only of same st as joining, sc in next st, (sc in back loop only of next st, sc in next st) around; join with sl st in first sc.

Note: Work first st of each rnd in same st as joining.

Rnd 3: Ch 1, sc in each st around; join with sl st in first sc. Fasten off.

Rnds 4 and 5: With C, rep Rnds 2 and 3. Fasten off.

Rnds 6 and 7: With D, rep Rnds 2 and 3. Fasten off.

Rnds 8 and 9: With E, rep Rnds 2 and 3. Fasten off.

Rnds 10 and 11: With F, rep Rnds 2 and 3. Fasten off.

Rnds 12 and 13: With G, rep Rnds 2 and 3. Fasten off.

Rnds 14 and 15: With H, rep Rnds 2 and 3. Fasten off.

Rnds 16 and 17: With A, rep Rnds 2 and 3. Fasten off.

Rnds 18 and 19: With B, rep Rnds 2 and 3. Fasten off.

Shape Crown (Top of Hat)

Rnd 20: With C, rep Rnd 2.

Rnd 21 (Decrease Rnd): Ch 1, *sc in next 5 sts, sc2tog; rep from * around; join with sl st in first sc – 60 sc at the end of this rnd. Fasten off.

Rnd 22: With D, rep Rnd 2.

Rnd 23 (Decrease Rnd): Ch 1, *sc in next 4 sts, sc2tog; rep from * around; join with sl st in first sc – 50 sc. Fasten off.

Rnd 24: With E, rep Rnd 2.

Rnd 25 (Decrease Rnd): Ch 1, *sc in next 3 sts, sc2tog; rep from * around; join with sl st in first sc – 40 sc. Fasten off.

Rnd 26: With F, rep Rnd 2.

Rnd 27 (Decrease Rnd): Ch 1, *sc in next 2 sts, sc2tog; rep from * around; join with sl st in first sc – 30 sc. Fasten off.

Rnd 28: With G, rep Rnd 2.

Rnd 29 (Decrease Rnd): Ch 1, *sc in next st, sc2tog; rep from * around; join with sl st in first sc – 20 sc. Fasten off.

Rnd 30: With H, rep Rnd 2.

Rnd 31 (Decrease Rnd): Ch 1, *sc2tog; rep from * around; join with sl st in first sc – 10 sc. Fasten off.

Rnd 32: With A, rep Rnd 2.

Fasten off, leaving a long yarn tail. Weave tail through sts of last rnd and pull to gather. Knot securely.

Earflaps

Place markers along lower edge of Hat for earflap placement as follows: Place first marker about 2" (5 cm) after joining. Place 2nd marker about 4" (10 cm) following first marker, 3rd marker about 5" (12.5 cm) following 2nd marker, and 4th marker about 4" (10 cm) following 3rd marker.

NOTES

1. The edge between the first and 2nd markers is for the first earflap and the edge between the 3rd and 4th markers is for the second earflap.
2. The edge of the Hat between the 2nd and 3rd markers is the front of the Hat.
3. To change color when working earflaps, work last st of old color to last yarn over. Yarn over with new color and draw through all loops on hook. Proceed with new color. Fasten off old color.

FIRST EARFLAP

Row 1 (WS): From WS, join A with sc at first marker, work 17 more sc evenly spaced across Hat edge to 2nd marker; leave remaining sts unworked – 18 sc. Change to H. Remove first and 2nd markers.

Work over 18 sts of first earflap only as follows:

Row 2: With H, ch 1, turn, *sc in back loop only of next st, sc in next st; rep from * across.

Row 3 (Decrease Row): With H, ch 1, turn, sc2tog, sc in each st across to last 2 sts, sc2tog – 16 sc. Change to G.

Row 4: With G, ch 1, turn, *sc in back loop only of next st, sc in next st; rep from * across.

Row 5: With G, ch 1, turn, sc in each st across. Change to F.

Rows 6 and 7: With F, rep Rows 2 and 3 – 14 sc. Change to E.

Rows 8 and 9: With E, rep Rows 4 and 5. Change to D.

Rows 10 and 11: With D, rep Rows 2 and 3 – 12 sc. Change to C.

Rows 12 and 13: With C, rep Rows 2 and 3 – 10 sc. Change to B.

Rows 14 and 15: With B, rep Rows 2 and 3 – 8 sc. Change to A.

Row 16: With A, rep Row 2. Fasten off.

SECOND EARFLAP

Work same as first earflap, working Row 1 between 3rd and 4th markers.

Finishing

EDGING

Rnd 1 (RS): From RS, join A with sc along lower edge of Hat. Work sc evenly spaced around lower edge of Hat and around outside edge of each earflap; join with sl st in beg sc. Fasten off.

TIES (make 2)

Note: Wind A into 2 separate balls before making ties.

Join 2 strands of A held tog with sl st in tip of first earflap, and ch for about 11" (28 cm). Fasten off. Rep on second earflap.

POM-POMS (make 3 – 1 each with D, F and G)

Following package directions, make small pom-poms. Tie D and G pom-poms to ends of ties. Tie F pom-pom to top of Hat.

Weave in ends.

CLUTCH

EASY

SIZE

About 9" (23 cm) wide x 5½" (14 cm) tall after folding

SHOPPING LIST

Yarn (Fine Weight) 2 FINE

LION BRAND® BONBONS® (Art. #601)

- ☐ #660 Celebrate - 1 pack **or** color of your choice

Crochet Hook

LION BRAND® crochet hook

- ☐ Size G-6 (4.25 mm)
  or size needed for gauge

Additional Supplies

- ☐ LION BRAND® stitch markers
- ☐ LION BRAND® large-eyed blunt needle
- ☐ 2 buttons, ¼-½" (6-13 mm) diameter

GAUGE

5 ripples = about 9" (23 cm) and
18 rows = about 4" (10 cm) in pattern.
BE SURE TO CHECK YOUR GAUGE.

TECHNIQUE EXPLANATION

Adjustable Ring Method

Wrap yarn around index finger. Insert hook into ring on finger, yarn over and draw up a loop. Carefully slip ring from finger and work the stitches of Rnd 1 (in pattern, below) into the ring. When Rnd 1 is complete, gently but firmly, pull tail to tighten center of ring.

NOTES

1. Clutch is worked in a ripple pattern, changing color on every other row.
2. The ripple pattern is easy to do, but it's important to remember that you may need to work several rows before the ripple pattern becomes clear.
3. The ripple pattern consists of alternating 3-sc peaks and 2 skipped st valleys. Take care to keep the peaks and valleys of each row aligned. 3 Sc are worked into the center sc of peaks and 2 sts are skipped at each valley. One st is skipped at each end to maintain a consistent stitch count.
4. To change color, work last st of old color to last yarn over. Yarn over with new color and draw through all loops on hook to complete st. Proceed with new color. Fasten off old color.

COLORS

Purple (A)	Pea Green (E)
Dark Blue (B)	Sparkling Peach (F)
Light Blue (C)	Red (G)
Emerald (D)	Hot Pink (H)

CLUTCH

With A, ch 64.

Row 1 (RS): Sc in 2nd ch from hook and in next 4 ch, (3 sc in next ch, sc in next 5 ch, sk next 2 ch, sc in next 5 ch) 4 times, 3 sc in next ch, sc in last 5 ch – 5 ripples at the end of this row.

Row 2: Ch 1, turn, sk first sc, sc in next 5 sts, (3 sc in next st, sc in next 5 sts, sk next 2 sts, sc in next 5 sts) 4 times, 3 sc in next st, sc in next 4 sts, sk next st, sc in last st. Change to B.

Rows 3 and 4: With B, rep Row 2. Change to C at the end of Row 4.

Rows 5-48: Rep Row 2, changing color every other row in following color sequence: (Work 2 rows each with C, D, E, F, G, H, A, B) 2 times, then work 2 rows each with C, D, E, F, G, H.
Change to A.

Row 49: With A, rep Row 2.

Row 50: With A, ch 5, sk first st, tr in next st, dc in next st, hdc in next st, sc in next st, sk next st, sl st in next st, sk next st, sc in next st, hdc in next st, dc in next st, tr in next st, (sk next 2 sts, tr in next st, dc in next st, hdc in next st, sc in next st, sk next st, sl st in next st, sk next st, sc in next st, hdc in next st, dc in next st, tr in next st) 4 times, tr in last st. Fasten off.

Finishing

ASSEMBLY

Place a marker on each side edge about 4½" (11.5 cm) from top edge. Fold down at markers. Join A with sc in one end of Row 1, working in ends of rows, sc evenly spaced across working through both thicknesses as necessary. Fasten off.
Join A with sc in corner at fold to work in ends of rows. Sc evenly spaced across side edge from fold to beg edge, working through both thicknesses as necessary. Fasten off.

BUTTON LOOPS

From RS, join A with sl st in 2nd "valley" of rippled edge, ch 7, sl st in same sp as joining. Fasten off. Rep to work a 2nd button loop in the 4th "valley."

BUTTON COVERS (make 2)

With H, make an adjustable ring.

Rnd 1: Ch 1, work 7 sc in ring; join with sl st in first sc – 7 sc.

Rnds 2 and 3: Ch 1, sc in each sc around; join with sl st in first sc. Fasten off, leaving a long yarn tail.

Place a button inside the cover. Thread yarn tail through sts of last rnd and pull to close around button. Use remaining tails to sew covered buttons to front of Clutch, opposite button loops.

Weave in ends.

FLOWER CHAIN SCARF

EASY

SIZE

About 4" x 48" (10 cm x 122 cm)

SHOPPING LIST

Yarn (Fine Weight) FINE 2

LION BRAND® BONBONS® (Art. #601)

- ☐ #630 Beach - 1 pack **or** color of your choice

Crochet Hooks

LION BRAND® crochet hook

- ☐ Size G-6 (4.25 mm)
  or size needed for gauge

Additional Supplies

- ☐ LION BRAND® large-eyed blunt needle

GAUGE

One Large Flower Motif = about 4" (10 cm) across.
One Small Flower Motif = about 2½" (6.5 cm) across.
BE SURE TO CHECK YOUR GAUGE.

TECHNIQUE EXPLANATION

Adjustable Ring Method

Wrap yarn around index finger. Insert hook into ring on finger, yarn over and draw up a loop. Carefully slip ring from finger and work the stitches of Rnd 1 (in pattern, below) into the ring. When Rnd 1 is complete, gently but firmly, pull tail to tighten center of ring.

NOTES

1. Scarf is made from 15 Flower Motifs; 8 Small Flower Motifs and 7 Large Flower Motifs.
2. Each Motif is worked in joined rnds with RS facing at all times. Do not turn at the beg of rnds.
3. Flower Motifs are arranged into a strip and sewn together.

COLORS

Purple (A)
Yellow (B)
Seafoam Green (C)
White (D)
Orange (E)
Turquoise (F)
Red (G)
Black (H)

LARGE FLOWER MOTIF (make 7 – 1 each with A, B, C, D, E, F, and G)

Make an adjustable ring.

Rnd 1 (RS): Ch 1, 8 sc in ring; join with sl st in first sc – 8 sc at the end of this rnd.

Rnd 2: Ch 3 (counts as first dc in this rnd and in all following rnds), dc in same st as joining, 2 dc in each st around; join with sl st in top of beg ch – 16 dc at the end of this rnd.

Rnd 3: Ch 1, sc in same st as joining, (ch 3, sk next st, sc in next st) around to last st, ch 3, sk last st; join with sl st in first sc – 8 sc and 8 ch-3 sps.

Rnd 4: (Sc, hdc, 3 dc, hdc, sc) in each ch-3 sp around; join with sl st in first sc – 8 (sc, hdc, 3 dc, hdc, sc) small petals.

Rnd 5: Sl st in next hdc, sl st in next dc, (sl st, ch 1, sc) in next dc (center dc of first 3-dc group), *ch 5, sk next 6 sts, sc in next dc (center dc of 3-dc group); rep from * around, ch 5, sk rem sts; join with sl st in first sc – 8 sc and 8 ch-5 sps.

Rnd 6: (Sc, hdc, 7 dc, hdc, sc) in each ch-5 sp around; join with sl st in first sc – 8 (sc, hdc, 7 dc, hdc, sc) large petals. Fasten off.

SMALL FLOWER MOTIF (make 8 – 1 each with A, B, C, D, E, F, G, and H)

Make same as Large Flower Motif through Rnd 4 – 8 small petals. Fasten off.

FINISHING

Arrange Flower Motifs into a strip in the following order: F-colored Small Flower, A-colored Large Flower, D-colored Small Flower, B-colored Large Flower, E-colored Small Flower, C-colored Large Flower, G-colored Small Flower, D-colored Large Flower, A-colored Small Flower, E-colored Large Flower, H-colored Small Flower, F-colored Large Flower, B-colored Small Flower, G-colored Large Flower, C-colored Small Flower. Keeping the Flowers arranged in a strip, rotate the Flowers so that the tip of one petal of each Large Flower lies between the tips of two petals of each of its neighboring Small Flowers. Using matching yarn, sew the tips together. Weave in ends.

DAY BAG

EASY +

SIZE

About 8½" x 11" (22 cm x 28 cm), not including handles

SHOPPING LIST

Yarn (Light Weight) LIGHT 3

LION BRAND® BONBONS® (Art. #601)

- ☐ #640 Nature - 1 pack **or** color of your choice

Crochet Hook

LION BRAND® crochet hook

- ☐ Size F-5 (3.75 mm)
  or size needed for gauge

Additional Supplies

- ☐ LION BRAND® large-eyed blunt needle

GAUGE

22 sts + 16 rows = 4" (10 cm) in pattern.

BE SURE TO CHECK YOUR GAUGE.

STITCH GUIDE

CROSSED HDC
(abbreviated cross-hdc)
Skip next st, hdc in next st, hdc in skipped st.

REVERSE SINGLE CROCHET
(abbreviated rev sc)
Single crochet worked from left to right (right to left, if left-handed). Insert hook into next stitch to the right (left), under loop on hook, and draw up a loop. Yarn over, draw through all loops on hook.

NOTES

1. Bag is worked in joined rnds beg at base.
2. After base is complete, color is changed every other rnd following Stripe Sequence.
3. To change color, work last st of old color to last yarn over. Yarn over with new color and draw through all loops on hook to complete st. Continue with new color. Fasten off old color.

COLORS

Chocolate Brown (A)
Tan (B)
Green (C)
Lightest Yellow (D)
Cream (E)
Dusty Rose (F)
Palest Lavender (G)
Purple (H)

STRIPE SEQUENCE

*Work 2 rnds with A, **2 rnds with B, 2 rnds with C, 2 rnds with D, 2 rnds with E, 2 rnds with F, 2 rnds with G, 2 rnds with H; rep from * 2 times total, then rep from ** once more for Stripe Sequence.

BAG

Base

Note: Do not turn at beg of rnds while working Base.

With A, ch 44.

Rnd 1 (RS): Sc in 2nd ch from hook and in each ch to last ch, 3 sc in last ch; working across opposite side of foundation ch, sc in next 41 ch, 2 sc in last ch (at base of first sc made); join with sl st in first sc – 88 sc.

Rnd 2: Ch 1, 2 sc in same st as joining, sc in next 41 sts, 2 sc in each of next 3 sts, sc in next 41 sts, 2 sc in each of last 2 sts; join with sl st in first sc – 94 sc.

Rnd 3: Ch 1, 2 sc in next st, sc in next 41 sts, 2 sc in next st, sc in next 4 sts, 2 sc in next st, sc in next 41 sts, 2 sc in next st, sc in next 4 sts; join with sl st in first sc – 98 sc.

Rnd 4: Ch 1, 2 sc in next st, sc in next 41 sts, 2 sc in next st, sc in next 6 sts, 2 sc in next st, sc in next 41 sts, 2 sc in next st, sc in next 6 sts; join with sl st in first sc – 102 sc.

Rnd 5: Ch 1, 2 sc in next st, sc in next 41 sts, 2 sc in next st, sc in next 8 sts, 2 sc in next st, sc in next 41 sts, 2 sc in next st, sc in next 8 sts; join with sl st in first sc – 106 sc.

Rnd 6: Ch 1, sc in same st as joining and in next 47 sts, 2 sc in next st, sc in next 52 sts, 2 sc in next st, sc in last 4 sts; join with sl st in first sc – 108 sc.

Rnd 7: Ch 1, working in back loops only, sc in each st around; join with sl st in first sc.

Sides

Note: Turn at beg of rnds while working Sides.

Rnd 8 (WS): Ch 2 (counts as hdc in this rnd and in all following rnds, serves as first part of last cross-hdc), turn, sk first st, *cross-hdc; rep from * to last st, sk last st (same st as joining of previous rnd), hdc in st skipped at beg of rnd (last cross-hdc completed); join with sl st in top of beg ch – 54 cross-hdc. Change to B.

Rnd 9: With B, ch 1, turn, sc in each st around; join with sl st in first ch.

Rnd 10: With B, ch 2, turn, sk first st, *cross-hdc; rep from * to last st, sk last st, hdc in st skipped at beg of rnd; join with sl st in top of beg ch.

Rnds 11-20: Rep last 2 rnds and continue to change color as in Stripe Sequence.
Note: The last 2 rnds you work should be worked with G. Change to H.

Rnd 21 (Increase Rnd): With H, ch 1, turn, 2 sc in first st, sc in next 42 sts, 2 sc in next st, sc in next 10 sts, 2 sc in next st, sc in next 42 sts, 2 sc in next st, sc in next 10 sts; join with sl st in first sc – 112 sts.

Rnd 22: With H, rep Rnd 10 – 56 cross-hdc.

Rnds 23-30: Rep Rnds 9 and 10 and continue to change color following Stripe Sequence. Change to E.

Rnd 31 (Increase Rnd): With E, ch 1, turn, 2 sc in first st, sc in next 44 sts, 2 sc next st, sc in next 10 sts, 2 sc in next st, sc in next 44 sts, 2 sc in next st, sc in next 10 sts; join with sl st in first sc – 116 sts.

Rnd 32: With E, rep Rnd 10 – 58 cross-hdc.

Rnds 33-38: Rep Rnds 9 and 10 and continue to change color following Stripe Sequence. Change to A.

Rnd 39 (Increase Rnd): With A, ch 1, turn, 2 sc in first st, sc in next 44 sts, 2 sc in next st, sc in next 12 sts, 2 sc in next st, sc in next 44 sts, 2 sc in next st, sc in next 12 sts; join with sl st in first sc – 120 sts.

Rnd 40: With A, rep Rnd 10 – 60 cross-hdc. Change to B.

Rnds 41 and 42: With B, rep Rnds 9 and 10. Change to C.

Top

Note: When Bag is complete, top edge will be folded over. Accordingly, the RS (outside) of the top edge is the WS (inside) of Bag.

Rnd 43 (RS of top of Bag): With C, ch 1, do not turn, sc in each st around; join with sl st in first ch.

Note: For Rnds 44-54, turn at the end of each rnd.

Rnd 44: With C, rep Rnd 10.

Rnds 45-54: Rep Rnds 9 and 10 and continue to change color following Stripe Sequence. At the end of Rnd 54, do not change color.

Edging

Rnd 55 (RS of top of Bag): With H, work rev sc in each st around; join with sl st in first ch. Fasten off.

HANDLES (make 2)

With E, ch 105.

Row 1 (RS): Sc in 2nd ch from hook and each ch across – 104 sts. Change to F.

Row 2: With F, ch 1, turn, sc in each st across. Change to G.

Row 3: With G, ch 1, turn, sc in each st across. Change to H.

Row 4: With H, ch 1, turn, sc in each st across. Change to A.

Row 5: With A, ch 1, turn, sc in each st across. Change to B.

Row 6: With B, ch 1, turn, sc in each st across. Change to C.

Row 7: With C, ch 1, turn, sc in each st across. Change to D.

Row 8: With D, ch 1, turn, sc in each st across. Do not fasten off.

Edging

Fold Handle lengthwise in half, bringing WS together. Ch 1, working through both thicknesses and into outside loops only of sts of last row and foundation ch at base of Row 1, sl st in each st across. Fasten off.

FINISHING

Fold top to outside, sew ends of Handles to inside of top (folded) edge of Bag, about 2" (5 cm) from sides. Weave in ends.

FINGER FUNNIES

EASY

SIZE

Each about 2½" (6.5 cm) tall

SHOPPING LIST

Yarn (Light Weight) LIGHT 3

LION BRAND® BONBONS® (Art. #601)

- ☐ #680 Crayons - 1 pack **or** color of your choice

Crochet Hook

LION BRAND® crochet hook

- ☐ Size I-9 (5.5 mm)
  or size needed for gauge

Additional Supplies

- ☐ LION BRAND® stitch marker
- ☐ LION BRAND® large-eyed blunt needle

GAUGE

16 sc + 20 rnds = about 4" (10 cm).
BE SURE TO CHECK YOUR GAUGE.

NOTES

1. Funnies are worked in rnds, then Hair and embroidered details are added.
2. Colors used in each of the sample Funnies are listed below – but feel free to use yarn colors as desired.
3. To change color, work last st of old color to last yarn over. Yarn over with new color and draw through both loops on hook to complete the st.

STRIPED FUNNIES

Sample 1: A = Bright Yellow, B = Hot Pink, C = Turquoise; hair = Bright Orange straight sts; mouth = Hot Pink.

Sample 2: A = Yellow-Orange, B = Green, C = Bright Orange; hair = Purple French knot buns with straight st bangs; mouth = Hot Pink.

Sample 3: A = Yellow-Orange, B = Turquoise, C = Green; hair = Hot Pink short loop ponytails with French knot bangs; mouth = Red.

With A, ch 2.

Rnd 1: Work 5 sc in 2nd ch from hook; do not join, work in continuous rnds. Place marker in first st for beg of rnd. Move marker up as each rnd is completed.

Rnd 2: Work 2 sc in each sc around – 10 sc at the end of this rnd.

Rnds 3-5: Sc in each st around. Change to B.

Note: When working Rnds 6-12, do not cut yarn between color changes, simply carry unused color up the inside of the Funnie.

Rnd 6: With B, sc in each st around. Change to C, but do not cut B.

Rnd 7: With C, sc in each st around. Change to B, but do not cut C.

Rnds 8-11: Rep Rnds 6 and 7 twice. At the end of Rnd 11, cut C.

Rnd 12: Rep Rnd 6. Fasten off.

COLOR BLOCK FUNNIES

Sample 1: A = Yellow-Orange, B = Purple, C = Hot Pink; hair = Green loops made into ponytails with straight st bangs; mouth = Red.

Sample 2: A = Yellow, B = Red, C = Purple; hair = Turquoise French knots; mouth = Hot Pink.

With A, ch 2.

Work Rnds 1-5 same as for Striped Funnie. Change to B.

Rnds 6-10: With B, sc in each st around. Change to C. Cut B.

Rnds 11 and 12: With C, sc in each st around. Fasten off.

FINISHING

Hair

Thread needle with a doubled strand of desired color yarn. Embroider French knots, straight sts or loops of varying lengths and sizes to create hair.
For loops, make a ½-2" (1.5-5 cm) loop of yarn and anchor that loop in place with a small st across base of loop.

Mouth

With desired color, embroider straight sts for mouth.
Weave in ends.

FLORAL COLLAR

EASY +

SIZE

About 17½" (44.5 cm) at neck edge

SHOPPING LIST

Yarn (Light Weight) LIGHT 3

LION BRAND® BONBONS® (Art. #601)

- ☐ #620 Pastels - 1 pack **or** color of your choice

Crochet Hook

LION BRAND® crochet hook

- ☐ Size H-8 (5 mm)

Additional Supplies

- ☐ LION BRAND® Pom-Pom Maker
- ☐ LION BRAND® large-eyed blunt needle

GAUGE

EXACT GAUGE IS NOT ESSENTIAL FOR THIS PROJECT.

TECHNIQUE EXPLANATION
Adjustable Ring Method

Wrap yarn around index finger. Insert hook into ring on finger, yarn over and draw up a loop. Carefully slip ring from finger and work the stitches of Rnd 1 (in pattern, below) into the ring. When Rnd 1 is complete, gently but firmly, pull tail to tighten center of ring.

NOTES

1. Collar, Flowers, and Leaves are crocheted separately then sewed together.
2. To change color, work last st of old color to last yarn over. Yarn over with new color and draw through all loops to complete st. Fasten off old color.

COLORS

Medium Blue (A)	Peach (E)
Sky Blue (B)	Pale Pink (F)
White (C)	Lavender (G)
Yellow (D)	Light Green (H)

COLLAR

With A, ch 71.

Row 1 (WS): Sc in 2nd ch from hook and in each ch across – 70 sc. Change to B.

Row 2: With B, ch 3 (counts as first dc in this row and in all following rows), turn, dc in each st across.

Row 3: Ch 1, turn, sc in first st, *ch 4, sk next 2 sts, sc in next st; rep from * across working the last sc in top of turning ch – 24 sc and 23 ch-4 sps. Change to C.

Row 4: With C, ch 3, turn, 4 dc in first ch-4 sp, *ch 2, sc in next ch-4 sp, ch 2, 4 dc in next ch-4 sp; rep from * across to last st, dc in last st – 50 dc, 11 sc, and 22 ch-2 sps.

Row 5: Ch 1, turn, sc in first st, *ch 4, sc in next ch-2 sp, ch 5, sc in next ch-2 sp; rep from * to last 5 sts, ch 4, sk next 4 sts, sc in last st (top of turning ch) – 24 sc, 12 ch-4 sps, and 11 ch-5 sps. Change to D.

Row 6: With D, ch 5 (counts as dc, ch 2), turn, sc in first ch-4 sp, *ch 2, 5 dc in next ch-5 sp, ch 2, sc in next ch-4 sp; rep from * across, ch 2, dc in last st – Eleven 5-dc groups and 24 ch-2 sps.

Row 7: Ch 1, turn, sc in first dc, sk first ch-2 sp, *ch 4, sc in next ch-2 sp, ch 5, sc in next ch-2 sp; rep from * across to turning ch-sp, ch 4, sc in 3rd ch of turning ch – 12 ch-4 sps and 11 ch-5 sps. Change to E.

Row 8: With E, ch 3, turn, (3 dc, ch 2, 3 dc) in next ch-4 sp (shell made), *ch 2, sc in next ch-5 sp, ch 2, (3 dc, ch 2, 3 dc) in next ch-4 sp; rep from * across, dc in last st – 12 shells.

Row 9: Ch 1, turn, sc in first dc, ch 4, (sc, ch 3, sc) in first ch-2 sp, *(ch 4, sc in next ch-2 sp) twice, ch 4, (sc, ch 3, sc) in next ch-2 sp; rep from * across, ch 4, sc in last dc (top of turning ch) – 48 sc, 12 ch-3 sps, and 35 ch-4 sps. Fasten off.

Flower 1 (make 12 – 6 each using F and G as 2nd color)

With E, make an adjustable ring.

Rnd 1 (RS): Ch 1, 11 sc in ring; change to 2nd color; join with sl st in beg ch.

Rnd 2: With 2nd color, (hdc, 2 dc, hdc) in first sc (petal made), *sc in next sc, (hdc, 2 dc, hdc) in next sc; rep from * 4 more times; join with sl st in first sc – 6 petals. Fasten off.

Flower 2 (make 6)

With E, make an adjustable ring.

Rnd 1 (RS): Ch 1, 11 sc in ring; change to F; join with sl st in beg ch.

Rnd 2: With F, ch 1, (hdc, 2 dc, hdc) in first sc (petal made); *change to G, sc in next sc, (hdc, 2 dc, hdc) in next sc; change to F, sc in next sc, (hdc, 2 dc, hdc) in next sc; rep from * once more; change to G, sc in next sc, (hdc, 2 dc, hdc) in next sc; join with sl st in first sc – 6 petals. Fasten off.

Flower 3 (make 5)

With D, make an adjustable ring.

Rnd 1 (RS): Ch 2, 6 dc in ring, change to C; join with sl st in top of beg ch.

Rnd 2: With C, *ch 6, sc in 2nd ch from hook, hdc in next ch, dc in next ch, hdc in next ch, sc in next ch (petal made), sl st in next dc of Rnd 1; rep from * 6 more times working last sl st in same st as joining sl st of Rnd 1 – 7 petals.

Flower 4 (make 12 – 6 each using A and B as 2nd color)

With D, ch 4; join with sl st in first ch to form a ring.

Rnd 1: Ch 1, 7 sc in ring; change to 2nd color; join with sl st in beg ch.

Rnd 2: With 2nd color, ch 4 (counts as tr), tr in next 7 sc; join with sl st in top of beg ch. Fasten off.

Stem 1 (make 6)

With H, ch 6.

First Leaf: Sc in 2nd ch from hook, hdc in next ch, dc in next ch, hdc in next ch, (sc, ch 2, sl st in 2nd ch from hook, sc) in last ch; working across opposite side of foundation ch, hdc in next ch, dc in next ch, hdc in next ch, sc in next ch, sl st in skipped ch at the beg of this rnd. Do not fasten off and do not turn.

First Half of Stem: Ch 6, sl st in 2nd ch from hook and in next 4 ch.
Second Half of Stem: Ch 6, sl st in 2nd ch from hook and in next 4 ch.

Second Leaf: Ch 6, sc in 2nd ch from hook, hdc in next ch, dc in next ch, hdc in next ch, dc in next ch, hdc in next ch, (sc, ch 1, sc) in last ch; working across opposite side of foundation ch, hdc in next ch, dc in next ch, hdc in next ch, sc in next ch, ch 2, sl st in 2nd ch from hook; join with sl st in first sc of 2nd leaf. Fasten off.

Stem 2 (make 5)

With H, ch 12 for stem.

Row 1: Sl st in 2nd ch from hook, sc in next 4 ch (first part of stem made), ch 4 for leaf, sc in 2nd ch from hook, hdc in next ch, dc in next ch (leaf made), sk next ch of stem ch, sl st in next 5 ch (stem completed). Fasten off.

Stem 3 (make 7)

With H, ch 7.

Row 1: Sl st in 2nd ch from hook and in next ch, (sl st, ch 3, sl st) in next ch (small leaf made), sl st in last 3 ch. Fasten off.

Tie

With 1 strand end of A and B held tog, make a ch about 50" (127 cm) long. Fasten off.

Finishing

Following Assembly Diagram, sew Flowers and Stems to Collar. Thread tie through sts of Row 2 of Collar beg under 2nd dc, *sk 3 dc, and thread under the next dc; rep from * across.

Pom-poms (make 2 – 1 each with A and B)

Following package directions, make a small pom-pom. Tie a pom-pom to each end of tie. Weave in ends.

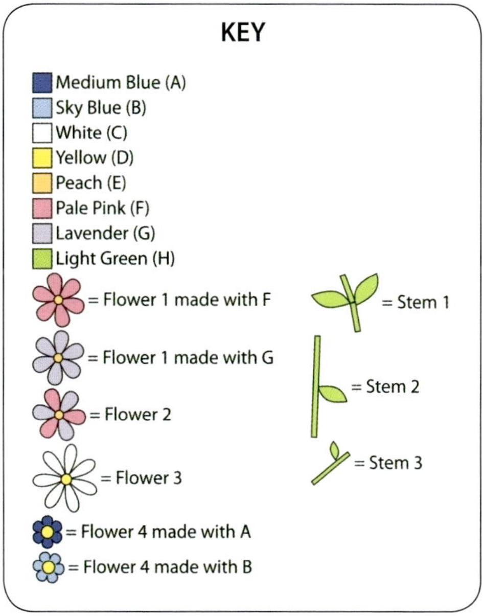

GRANNY SQUARE SCARF & HAT

EASY

SIZE

Scarf

About 4" x 58" (10 cm x 147.5 cm)

Hat

Finished circumference:

About 19" (48.5 cm), will stretch to fit a range of sizes.

SHOPPING LIST

Yarn (Fine Weight) FINE 2

LION BRAND® BONBONS® (Art. #601)

☐ #650 Party - 2 packs **or** color of your choice

Crochet Hook

LION BRAND® crochet hook

☐ Size G-6 (4.25 mm)

or size needed for gauge

Additional Supplies

☐ LION BRAND® large-eyed blunt needle

GAUGE

One Square = about 3¼" x 3¼" (8.5 cm x 8.5 cm).
BE SURE TO CHECK YOUR GAUGE.

NOTES

1. Scarf is made from 17 Squares sewed together.
2. Hat beg by making and sewing together 6 Squares. Top of Hat is worked beg around one edge of circle of Squares. Lower edge of Hat is worked beg around other edge of circle of Squares.
3. Squares are worked in the round, with RS always facing.
4. The color is changed on every round of each Square. Change color by fastening off old color and drawing up a loop of new color in a corner ch-2 space.

COLORS

Bronze (A)
Red (B)
Copper (C)
Gold (D)
Sparkling Taupe (E)
Magenta (F)
Teal (G)
Dark Purple (H)

SCARF

Square I (make 5)

With C, ch 6; join with sl st in first ch to form a ring.

Rnd 1 (RS): Ch 3 (counts as first dc in this rnd and in all following rnds), 2 dc in ring, ch 2, (3 dc in ring, ch 2) 3 times; join with sl st in top of beg ch – 12 dc and 4 ch-2 sps. Fasten off.

Rnd 2: From RS, draw up a loop of B in any ch-2 sp, ch 3, (2 dc, ch 2, 3 dc) in same ch-2 sp (first corner made), *ch 1, (3 dc, ch 2, 3 dc) in next ch-2 sp (corner made), ch 1; rep from * 2 more times; join with sl st in top of beg ch – 24 dc, 4 corner ch-2 sps, and 4 ch-1 sps at the end of this rnd. Fasten off.

Rnd 3: From RS, draw up a loop of A in any corner ch-2 sp, ch 3, (2 dc, ch 2, 3 dc) in same ch-2 sp, *ch 1, 3 dc in next ch-1 sp, ch 1, (3 dc, ch 2, 3 dc) in next corner ch-2 sp; rep from * 2 more times, ch 1, 3 dc in next ch-1 sp, ch 1; join with sl st in top of beg ch – 36 dc, 4 corner ch-2 sps, and 8 ch-1 sps. Fasten off.

Rnd 4: From RS, draw up a loop of D in any corner ch-2 sp, ch 3, (2 dc, ch 2, 3 dc) in same ch-2 sp, *(ch 1, 3 dc in next ch-1 sp) twice, ch 1, (3 dc, ch 2, 3 dc) in next corner ch-2 sp; rep from * 2 more times, (ch 1, 3 dc in next ch-1 sp) twice, ch 1; join with sl st in top of beg ch – 48 dc, 4 corner ch-2 sps, and 12 ch-1 sps. Fasten off.

Square II (make 4)

Make same as Square I in the following Color Sequence: Work 1 rnd each with H, G, F, E.

Square III (make 4)

Make same as Square I in the following Color Sequence: Work 1 rnd each with D, A, B, C.

Square IV (make 4)

Make same as Square I in the following Color Sequence: Work 1 rnd each with E, F, G, H.

FINISHING

Arrange Squares into a strip in the following order: *Square I, Square II, Square III, Square IV; rep from * 3 more times, then add the last Square I.

Sew Squares tog using a color to match the center color of one of the Squares being joined.

Border

Note: To change color when working border, work last st of old color to last yarn over. Yarn over with new color and draw through all loops on hook to complete st. Fasten off old color. Proceed with new color.

From RS, draw up a loop of F in any corner ch-2 sp, so that you are ready to work across a long edge.

Rnd 1 (RS): Ch 3, 2 dc in same corner ch-2 sp, *(ch 1, 3 dc in next ch-1 sp or next join between Squares) across long edge to next corner ch-2 sp, ch 1, (3 dc, ch 2, 3 dc) in corner ch-2 sp, (ch 1, 3 dc in next ch-1 sp) across short edge to next corner ch-2 sp **, ch 1, 3 dc in corner ch-2 sp; ch 1, change to C, 3 dc in same corner ch-2 sp; rep from * to ** working across other long edge and short edge, ch 1, 3 dc in same corner as joining, ch 1; join with sl st in top of beg ch. Fasten off.

From RS, draw up a loop of G in first corner ch-2 sp (where F-colored long edge beg).

Rnd 2: Work same as Rnd 1, changing to B in 3rd corner ch-2 sp. Fasten off.
Weave in ends.

HAT

Note: Follow Scarf pattern to make Squares.

Squares (make 6)

Make 2 each of Squares II and III, and one each of Squares I and IV.

Arrange Squares into a strip in the following order: Square I, Square II, Square III, Square II, Square III, Square IV. Sew Squares tog using a color to match the center color of one of the Squares being joined, then sew first and last Squares of strip together to make a ring.

Crown (Top of Hat)

From RS, draw up a loop of F in any ch-1 sp on one edge of ring.

Rnd 1: Ch 3 (counts as first dc in this rnd and in all following rnds), 2 dc in same ch-1 sp, *ch 1, 3 dc in next ch-1 sp or next join between Squares (do not work into the corner ch-2 sps of the Squares); rep from * around, ch 1; join with sl st in top of beg ch – Twenty-four 3-dc groups. Fasten off.

Rnd 2: From RS, draw up a loop of G in any ch-1 sp, ch 3, 2 dc in same ch-1 sp, *ch 1, 3 dc in next ch-1 sp; rep from * around, ch 1; join with sl st in top of beg ch. Fasten off.

Rnd 3: With H, rep Rnd 2. Fasten off.

Rnd 4: With E, rep Rnd 2. Fasten off.

Rnd 5: With C, rep Rnd 2. Fasten off.

Rnd 6: From RS, draw up a loop of B in any ch-1 sp, ch 3, 2 dc in same ch-1 sp, (ch 1, 3 dc in next ch-1 sp) twice, ch 1, dc in next ch-1 sp, *(ch 1, 3 dc in next ch-1 sp) 3 times, ch 1, dc in next ch-1 sp; rep from * around, ch 1; join with sl st in top of beg ch – Eighteen 3-dc groups and 6 dc. Fasten off.

Rnd 7: From RS, draw up a loop of A in any dc not part of a 3-dc group, ch 3, 2 dc in same dc, ch 1, sk next ch-1 sp, (3 dc in next ch-1 sp, ch 1) twice, *sk next ch-1 sp, 3 dc in next dc, ch 1, sk next ch-1 sp, (3 dc in next ch-1 sp, ch 1) twice; rep from * around; join with sl st in top of beg ch – Eighteen 3-dc groups. Fasten off.

Rnd 8: From RS, draw up a loop of D in any ch-1 sp, ch 3, 2 dc in same ch-1 sp, ch 1, 3 dc in next ch-1 sp, ch 1, dc in next ch-1 sp, *(ch 1, 3 dc in next ch-1 sp) twice, ch 1, dc in next ch-1 sp; rep from * around, ch 1; join with sl st in top of beg ch – Twelve 3-dc groups and 6 dc. Fasten off.

Rnd 9: From RS, draw up a loop of H in any dc not a part of a 3-dc group, ch 3, 2 dc in same dc, ch 1, sk next ch-1 sp, 3 dc in next ch-1 sp, *ch 1, sk next ch-1 sp, 3 dc in next dc, ch 1, sk next ch-1 sp, 3 dc in next ch-1 sp; rep from * around, ch 1; join with sl st in top of beg ch – Twelve 3-dc groups. Fasten off.

Rnd 10: From RS, draw up a loop of G in any ch-1 sp, ch 3, 2 dc in same ch-1 sp, ch 1, dc in next ch-1 sp, *ch 1, 3 dc in next ch-1 sp, ch 1, dc in next ch-1 sp; rep from * around, ch 1; join with sl st in top of beg ch – Six 3-dc groups and 6 dc. Fasten off.

Rnd 11: From RS, draw up a loop of F in any dc not a part of a 3-dc group, ch 3, 2 dc in same dc, ch 1, *sk next 2 ch-1 sps, 3 dc in next dc, ch 1; rep from * around, sk last 2 ch-1 sps; join with sl st in top of beg ch – Six 3-dc groups. Fasten off.

Rnd 12: From RS, draw up a loop of E in any ch-1 sp, ch 4, *dc in next ch-1 sp, ch 1; rep from * around; join with sl st in 3rd ch of beg ch – 6 dc.
Fasten off, leaving a long yarn tail. Thread yarn tail through sts of last rnd and pull to gather. Knot securely.

Lower Edging

Working around remaining edge of ring of Squares, work same as Rnds 1-3 of Crown (Top of Hat). Fasten off.

FINISHING

Weave in ends.

STRIPED WRISTERS

EASY

SIZE

Finished circumference:
About 8" (20.5 cm)
Finished Length: About 6½" (16.5 cm)

SHOPPING LIST

Yarn (Light Weight) LIGHT 3

LION BRAND® BONBONS® (Art. #601)

- ☐ #680 Crayons - 1 pack **or** color of your choice

Crochet Hook

LION BRAND® crochet hook

- ☐ Size H-8 (5 mm)
  or size needed for gauge

Additional Supplies

- ☐ LION BRAND® Pom-Pom Maker
- ☐ LION BRAND® large-eyed blunt needle

GAUGE

16 sc + 17 rows = 4" (10 cm).
BE SURE TO CHECK YOUR GAUGE.

STITCH GUIDE

SINGLE CROCHET 2 TOGETHER (abbreviated sc2tog)

(Insert hook in next st and draw up a loop) twice, yarn over and draw through all 3 loops on hook – 1 st decreased.

NOTE

Wristers are worked in joined rnds with a thumb opening made by working back and forth in rows.

COLORS

Bright Green (A)
Royal Purple (B)
Bright Orange (C)
Tangerine (D)
Yellow (E)
True Red (F)
Aqua Blue (G)
Hot Pink (H)

WRISTER (make 2)

With A, ch 32; taking care not to twist ch, join with sl st in first ch to form a ring. Fasten off.

Rnd 1 (RS): Join B with sc in same ch as joining, sc in each ch around; join with sl st in first sc – 32 sc.

Rnd 2: With B, ch 1, sc in same st as joining and in each sc around; join with sl st in first sc. Fasten off.

Rnd 3: From RS and working in back loops only, join C with sc in same st as joining, sc in each sc around; join with sl st in first sc.

Rnd 4: With C, rep Rnd 2. Fasten off.

Rnds 5-18: Rep last 2 rnds 7 more times, changing color as follows: Work 2 rnds with D, 2 rnds with E, 2 rnds with F, 2 rnds with G, 2 rnds with H, 2 rnds with A, and 2 rnds with B. Fasten off.

Rnd 19: With C, rep Rnd 3.

Thumb Opening

NOTES

1. To leave an opening for thumb, work back and forth in rows without joining at end of rows.
2. To change color at the end of a row, work last st to last yarn over. Yarn over with new color and draw through all loops on hook to complete st. Proceed with new color.

Row 20: With C, sc in same st as joining and in each sc around; do not join. Change to D. Fasten off C.

Rows 21 and 22: With D, ch 1, turn, sc in each st across. Change to E at the end of Row 22. Fasten off D.

Row 23: With E, ch 1, turn, sc in each st across.

Note: Thumb opening is now complete. Continue in joined rnds.

Rnd 24: With E, ch 1, turn, sc in each st across; join with sl st in first sc. Fasten off.

Rnds 25 and 26: With F, rep Rnds 3 and 4. Fasten off.

Rnd 27: With G, rep Rnd 3.

Shape Top of Wrister

Rnd 28 (Decrease Rnd): With G, ch 1, sc in same st as joining, sc in next 5 sc, sc2tog, (sc in next 6 sc, sc2tog) 3 times; join with sl st in first sc – 28 sc at the end of this rnd. Fasten off.

Thumb

Rnd 1 (RS): From RS, join C with sc anywhere along thumb opening, work 9 more sc evenly spaced around opening; join with sl st in first sc – 10 sc.

Rnd 2: With C, ch 1, sc in same st as joining and in each sc around; join with sl st in first sc. Fasten off.

Rnd 3: From RS and working in back loops only, join A with sc in same st as joining, sc in each sc around; join with sl st in first sc.

Rnd 4: With A, rep Rnd 2. Fasten off.

FINISHING

Lower Edging: From RS, join A with sl st anywhere along wrist edge of Wrister, sl st evenly spaced around. Fasten off. Weave in ends.

Pom-poms (make 2 – 1 each with G and H)

Following package directions, make 2 small pom-poms. Tie a pom-pom to wrist edge of each Wrister, opposite thumb.

V-SHAPED STRIPED SHAWL

EASY

SIZE

About 44" (112 cm) wide x 21½" (54.5 cm) long at widest and longest points.

SHOPPING LIST

Yarn (Light Weight) LIGHT 3

LION BRAND® BONBONS® (Art. #601)

- ☐ #620 Pastels - 1 pack
- ☐ #610 Brights - 1 pack

or colors of your choice

Crochet Hook

LION BRAND® crochet hook

- ☐ Size I-9 (5.5 mm)

or size needed for gauge

Additional Supplies

- ☐ LION BRAND® stitch marker
- ☐ LION BRAND® large-eyed blunt needle

GAUGE

12 sts (four 3-dc groups) + 6 rows = about 4" (10 cm) in pattern.

EXACT GAUGE IS NOT ESSENTIAL FOR THIS PROJECT.

NOTES

1. Shawl is worked in rows with RS facing at all times.
2. Color is changed every row. Fasten off old color and join new color to beg ch of row to beg next row.

COLORS

White (A)	Purple (I)
Pastels Yellow (B)	Pink (J)
Brights Yellow (C)	Magenta (K)
Orange (D)	Light Green (L)
Peach (E)	Lime (M)
Orange-Red (F)	Turquoise (N)
Pale Pink (G)	Sky Blue (O)
Lavender (H)	Medium Blue (P)

SHAWL

With A, ch 5.

Row 1 (RS): (3 dc, ch 2, 3 dc, ch 1, dc) in 5th ch from hook (beg ch counts as dc, ch 1) – Two 3-dc groups at the end of this row. Fasten off.

Row 2: From RS, join B with sl st in 4th ch of beg ch, ch 4 (counts as dc, ch 1 in this row and in all following rows), 3 dc in first ch-1 sp (formed by beg ch of previous row), ch 1, (3 dc, ch 2, 3 dc) in next ch-2 sp, ch 1, 3 dc in next ch-1 sp, ch 1, dc in last dc – Four 3-dc groups at the end of this row. Fasten off.

Row 3: From RS, join C with sl st in 3rd ch of beg ch of previous row, ch 4, 3 dc in first ch-1 sp, ch 1, 3 dc in next ch-1 sp, ch 1, (3 dc, ch 2, 3 dc) in next ch-2 sp, (ch 1, 3 dc in next ch-1 sp) 2 times, ch 1, dc in last dc – Six 3-dc groups at the end of this row. Fasten off.

Row 4: From RS, join D with sl st in 3rd ch of beg ch of previous row, ch 4, 3 dc in first ch-1 sp, (ch 1, 3 dc in next ch-1 sp) 2 times, ch 1, (3 dc, ch 2, 3 dc) in next ch-2 sp, (ch 1, 3 dc in next ch-1 sp) 3 times, ch 1, dc in last dc – Eight 3-dc groups at the end of this row. Fasten off.

Row 5: From RS, join E with sl st in 3rd ch of beg ch of previous row, ch 4, 3 dc in first ch-1 sp, *ch 1, 3 dc in next ch-1 sp; rep from * to center ch-2 sp, ch 1, (3 dc, ch 2, 3 dc) in center ch-2 sp, **ch 1, 3 dc in next ch-1 sp; rep from ** across, ch 1, dc in last dc – Ten 3-dc groups at the end of this row. Fasten off.

Rows 6-26: Rep last rnd 21 more times, changing color as in following color sequence: Work 1 row each with F, A, G, H, I, J, K, L, M, N, O, P, A, B, C, D, E, F, G, H, I – Fifty-two 3-dc groups at the end of Row 26. Fasten off.

Row 27: From RS, join J with sl st in 3rd ch of beg ch of previous row, ch 3 (counts as hdc, ch 1 in this row and in all following rows), hdc in first ch-1 sp, hdc in each st and ch-1 sp to center ch-2 sp, (2 hdc, ch 2, 2 hdc) in center ch-2 sp, hdc in each st and ch-1 sp across, ch 1, hdc in last dc – 214 hdc, 2 ch-1 sps, and 1 center ch-2 sp. Fasten off.

Row 28: From RS, join K with sl st in 2nd ch of beg ch of previous row, ch 3, hdc in first ch-1 sp, hdc in each hdc to center ch-2 sp, (2 hdc, ch 2, 2 hdc) in center ch-2 sp, hdc in each st to last ch-1 sp, hdc in last ch-1 sp, ch 1, hdc in last st – 220 hdc, 2 ch-1 sps, and 1 center ch-2 sp. Fasten off.

Row 29: From RS, join L with sl st in 2nd ch of beg ch of previous row, ch 3, hdc in first ch-1 sp, hdc in each st to center ch-2 sp, 4 hdc in center ch-2 sp, place a marker in the sp between the center 2 hdc of the 4-hdc just made to indicate center point, hdc in each st to last ch-1 sp, hdc in last ch-1 sp, ch 1, hdc in last st – 226 hdc, and 2 ch-1 sps. Fasten off.

Row 30: From RS, join M with sl st in 2nd ch of beg ch, ch 5, sl st in first ch-1 sp, *ch 5, sk next 2 sts, sl st in next st; rep from * to 2 sts before last ch-1 sp, ch 5, sk next 2 sts, sl st in last ch-1 sp, ch 5, sl st in last hdc – 77 ch-5 sps. Fasten off. Move center point marker to ch-5 sp over center point.

Row 31: From RS, join N with sl st in 2nd ch of beg ch, ch 5, sl st in first ch-sp, *ch 5, sl st in next ch-5 sp; rep from * across working last sl st in last ch-5 sp, ch 5, sl st in 3rd ch of last ch-5 sp – 78 ch-5 sps. Fasten off. Move center point marker to ch-5 sp over center point.

Row 32: From RS, join O with sl st in 2nd ch of beg ch, ch 5, sl st in first ch-sp, *ch 5, sl st in next ch-5 sp; rep from * across to center point, ch 7, sl st in next ch-5 sp, **ch 5, sl st in next ch-5 sp; rep from ** across working last sl st in last ch-5 sp, ch 5, sl st in 3rd ch of last ch-5 sp – 79 ch-sps. Fasten off. Remove center point marker.

Row 33: From RS, join P with sl st in 2nd ch of beg ch, ch 5, sl st in first ch-sp, *ch 5, sl st in next ch-5 sp; rep from * across to center ch-7 sp, ch 5, (sl st, ch 5, sl st) in center ch-7 sp, **ch 5, sl st in next ch-5 sp; rep from ** across working last sl st in last ch-5 sp, ch 5, sl st in 3rd ch of last ch-5 sp – 81 ch-sps. Fasten off.

FINISHING

Weave in ends.

GENERAL INSTRUCTIONS

ABBREVIATIONS

beg = begin(ning)(s)
ch = chain
ch-sp(s) = chain space(s) previously made
cm = centimeter
hdc = half double crochet
dc = double crochet
hdc = half double crochet
mm = millimeters
rep = repeat
RS = right side
rnd(s) = round(s)
sc = single crochet
sk = skip
sl st = slip stitch
sp(s) = space(s)
st(s) = stitch(es)
tog = together
tr = treble (triple) crochet
WS = wrong side

CROCHET TERMINOLOGY		
UNITED STATES		INTERNATIONAL
slip stitch (slip st)	=	single crochet (sc)
single crochet (sc)	=	double crochet (dc)
half double crochet (hdc)	=	half treble crochet (htr)
double crochet (dc)	=	treble crochet(tr)
treble crochet (tr)	=	double treble crochet (dtr)
double treble crochet (dtr)	=	triple treble crochet (ttr)
triple treble crochet (tr tr)	=	quadruple treble crochet (qtr)
skip	=	miss

* — When you see an asterisk used within a pattern row, the symbol indicates that later you will be told to repeat a portion of the instruction. Most often the instructions will say, repeat from * so many times.

( ) or **[ ]** — Set off a short number of stitches that are repeated or indicate additional information.

— When you see – followed by a number of stitches, this tells you how many stitches you will have at the end of a row or round.

GAUGE

Never underestimate the importance of gauge. Achieving the correct gauge assures that the finished size of your piece matches the finished size given in the pattern.

CROCHET HOOKS																
U.S.	B-1	C-2	D-3	E-4	F-5	G-6	H-8	I-9	J-10	K-10½	L-11	M/N-13	N/P-15	P/Q	Q	S
Metric - mm	2.25	2.75	3.25	3.5	3.75	4	5	5.5	6	6.5	8	9	10	15	16	19

BEGINNER	Projects for first-time crocheters using basic stitches. Minimal shaping.
EASY	Projects using yarn with basic stitches, repetitive stitch patterns, simple color changes, and simple shaping and finishing.
INTERMEDIATE	Projects using a variety of techniques, such as basic lace patterns or color patterns, mid-level shaping and finishing.
EXPERIENCED	Projects with intricate stitch patterns, techniques and dimension, such as non-repeating patterns, multi-color techniques, fine threads, small hooks, detailed shaping and refined finishing.

CHECKING YOUR GAUGE

Work a swatch that is at least 4" (10 cm) square. Use the suggested hook size and the number of stitches given. If your swatch is larger than 4" (10 cm), you need to work it again using a smaller hook; if it is smaller than 4" (10 cm), try it with a larger hook. This might require a swatch or two to get the exact gauge given in the pattern.

METRICS

As a handy reference, keep in mind that 1 ounce = approximately 28 grams and 1" = 2.5 centimeters.

TERMS

continue in this way or as established — Once a pattern is set up (established), the instructions may tell you to continue in the same way.

fasten off — To end your piece, you need to simply pull the yarn through the last loop left on the hook. This keeps the last stitch intact and prevents the work from unraveling.

right side — Refers to the front of the piece.

Yarn Weight Symbol & Names	LACE 0	SUPER FINE 1	FINE 2	LIGHT 3	MEDIUM 4	BULKY 5	SUPER BULKY 6
Type of Yarns in Category	Fingering, 10-count crochet thread	Sock, Fingering Baby	Sport, Baby	DK, Light Worsted	Worsted, Afghan, Aran	Chunky, Craft, Rug	Bulky, Roving
Crochet Gauge* Ranges in Single Crochet to 4" (10 cm)	32-42 double crochets**	21-32 sts	16-20 sts	12-17 sts	11-14 sts	8-11 sts	5-9 sts
Advised Hook Size Range	Steel*** 6,7,8 Regular hook B-1	B-1 to E-4	E-4 to 7	7 to I-9	I-9 to K-10.5	K-10.5 to M-13	M-13 and larger

*GUIDELINES ONLY: The chart above reflects the most commonly used gauges and hook sizes for specific yarn categories.

** Lace weight yarns are usually crocheted on larger-size hooks to create lacy openwork patterns. Accordingly, a gauge range is difficult to determine. Always follow the gauge stated in your pattern.

*** Steel crochet hooks are sized differently from regular hooks–the higher the number the smaller the hook, which is the reverse of regular hook sizing.

We have made every effort to ensure that these instructions are accurate and complete. We cannot, however, be responsible for human error, typographical mistakes, or variations in individual work.